Archaeological Sites of Yucatan

Dante

Introduction

"Life is not the one you lived,
but rather the one you remember
and how you remember it in the telling."
GABRIEL GARCÍA MÁRQUEZ

From the day the daguerreotype first appeared, it was predicted that it would change our vision of the world. How could this not happen, if no-one could remain indifferent faced with the beauty and "fidelity" of the image?

By the second half of the 19th century, all Europe was invaded by photography: everyone was fascinated by it, from royalty to the poorest workers; countries, cities, castles, towns and villages were photographed. So were social events, both public and private: baptisms, weddings, funerals, it was all captured on daguerreotype, dry plates, rigid plates, until the coming of plastic.

The same thing happened on the American continent, and Yucatan was no exception: from 1842 onwards, the light reflected from imposing Mayan constructions began to be captured by the daguerreotype. By 1860, the Yucatecans had already learned the art of photography and the first businesses promoting it came into being. The charms of the women of the Mayab began to be recorded on the first photographers' plates. Thus Yucatan fell in love with photography.

Her lovers, the Espinosa Rendón family (1860–1883) and the Guerra family (c.1877–1980), made photography into a tradition which is still practiced by our photographers.

The Guerras' business lasted more than a hundred years in the city market, and since portrait photography was the most common genre, the physiognomy of Yucatan at that time was portrayed: every Yucatecan (maybe 80%) was photographed by this family. Today there are a little over five hundred thousand images preserved in the "Pedro Guerra" photo archive, in the Faculty of Anthropology of the Autonomous University of Yucatan.

Mr. Guerra and his son also traveled the state with their camera, recording people, villages, haciendas, monuments, churches, archaeological zones and everything they could. It didn't matter how far or inhospitable the place: the shot had to be taken, a piece taken from the canvas of reality and hidden in the camera.

These images bear witness to those travels; and now, thanks to Dante Publishing and the Autonomous University of Yucatan, can be admired in this book and appreciated in all their glory and beauty.

Waldemaro Concha Vargas.

Prologue

One of the major attractions in Yucatan, and a great part of its beauty, are its pre-Hispanic Mayan sites, ever surrounded by an aura of mystery.

The Archaeological Sites of Yucatan contains images of part of that pre-Conquest era, through the lenses of the first photographers. For many years, scholars believed that pre-Hispanic Mayan settlements were merely ceremonial centers inhabited by priests and surrounded by peasants living scattered throughout the countryside.

Today, we know that they were complex cities in which governors, artists, artisans and the people of varying social ranks lived together.

The ruling elite constructed residential, political and religious edifices, solidly built and richly decorated with stone carvings, stucco and paint.

The monumental architecture should thus be appreciated not only for its artistic qualities, but also as historical document, the reading of which allows us a glimpse at the society's way of life and of perceiving the world around it.

However, to understand Mayan architecture it is necessary to understand its context.

The Maya conceived of a universe divided into three levels: the upper, the middle and and the lower level. The upper level, corresponding to the celestial regions; the middle level, inhabited by men; and the lower level or underworld, the Xibalbá of the Popol Vuj (or Popol Vuh); and the

three were linked together by the sacred ceiba tree. The humans could pass through the three levels of the universe by means of rituals, although there also existed what we could call portals in the form of caves and cenotes, and even buildings such as ball courts, one of the best examples of which is the Ball Court at Chichén Itzá.

The four compass points also played an important role, and each one of these, had a particular color and associated deities.

The sacred geography also included some mountains, water tables, caves, trees and animals; and humans reproduced these features in their buildings: the elevated temples were an artificial expression of the mountain; and its counterpart, the cavern, was represented by their entrances.

This can be seen in the so-called Chenes Temple on the Sorcerer's Pyramid at Uxmal, whose entrance is designed like the jaws of the monster Uitz.

Thus both the form of the buildings and their location and orientation formed part of their significance.

The images presented in this book correspond mainly to the Late Classical period, around 800 to 1000 A.D., from two of the greatest pre-Hispanic cities in the north of the Yucatan peninsula: Uxmal and Chichén Itzá.

Church and Annexe to the Temple of the Altarpieces, Chichén Itzá.

Uxmal

Uxmal, located in the Puuc or hill zone, was a city whose center, like that of other Mayan settlements, was surrounded by a wall. Its architecture constitutes one of the finest examples of the style also called Puuc, which −in its sub-styles known as Junquillo, Mosaic and Late Uxmal− demonstrates the talent of its architects and sculptors, in a kind of stone filigree that crowns the smooth walls of the lower part of the buildings.

Among the most outstanding buildings at Uxmal is the Sorcerer's Temple, which was magically constructed, according to the legend, in a single night by a dwarf who went on to become one of the city's greatest rulers.

In fact, the building shows various different stages of construction, one of which was of elongated galleries, as in a palace. The Chenes Temple, located on the rear side, facing the Birds' Quadrangle, has the open jaws of the Earth Monster also found at other sites such as Hochob, Tabasqueño and Ek' Balam.

At Uxmal we also find the Nuns' Quadrangle, an arbitrary name derived from its large number of cell-like rooms.

This complex is made up of four buildings around a courtyard, situated at different elevations and with different motifs, among which we can make out some plumed serpents, owls, masks and dignitaries, and representations of thatch houses on geometric backgrounds.

The Governor's Palace, a marvellous example of Late Uxmal style, stands on an imposing artificial platform facing East towards places such as Nohcacab and Kabah, which were related to Uxmal and connected to it by a sac bé or "white road".

After ascending the staircase that leads to the front terrace, we can see the finely carved stones of the smooth walls which support cornices, and friezes with geometric motifs, borders and mosaic masks. The stone vaults of this building achieve truly remarkable height and elegance.

In the same Puuc style is Chacmultún, a site where we can admire the elaborate architectonic design manifested in the various multi-floor palaces, these are richly decorated with pillars and mural paintings.

Chichén Itzá

The city of Chichén Itzá extends over more than 20 square kilometers. It was a majestic capital that attained great military and economic power, as well as notable ritual importance, even after it was abandoned, as is shown both in early colonial chronicles and also by archaeological objects recovered from the Sacred Cenote, including various offerings of gold, ceramic, jade and other materials from distant places and various eras.

Chichén Itzá has attracted the attention of researchers, among other reasons, because of the presence of two architectonic styles: the Pure Flourishing and the Modified Flourishing. The former has been considered very similar to the Puuc style, as can be seen in buildings such as the Church, the Painted House, the Nuns and the Nuns' Annexe, where the smooth walls with mosaic designs are reminiscent of distant Uxmal.

The Modified Flourishing style, also known as Mayan-Toltec, dominates at Chichén Itzá and is represented by the large temples with sloping sides, such as the Castle and the Ossuary, the triple entrances supported by serpentine columns, the spacious pillared rooms, the free-standing statues such as the Chac Mol and the standard-bearer, and the imposing carved presence of jaguars, eagles, processions of warriors and the Plumed Serpent, Kukulkán, presiding over the entrances to the most important buildings. Ritual and war are fused in the great Ball Court and the wall of skulls on the Tzompantli, both of an impressive and captivating beauty that produces a chill in the observer.

It was once believed that the two architectonic styles at Chichén Itzá were the result of the superimposition on a Mayan period of a later Toltec invasion, but modern research describes the Itzá capital as a cosmopolitan city whose political and commercial relations with other sites in the Mayan area and MesoAmerica −the Gulf Coast and the center of Mexico −brought about a characteristic style, to the extent that the clear-cut architectonic division made by researchers may not coincide with the perception of the city's inhabitants. The images in this book are an invitation: the past awaits in every stone, ready to tell us the ancient history of the Maya.

Lilia Fernández.

East side of the Nuns' Quadrangle, Uxmal.

The Church, Chichén Itzá.

West side of the Observatory, Chichén Itzá.

Akab Dzib, Chichén Itzá.

Northwest corner of the Temple of Warriors, Chichén Itzá.

Plaza of a Thousand Columns, south side of the Temple of Warriors, Chichén Itzá. In the background the Castle and Ball Court.

Annexe of the Nunnery and
the Church, Chichén Itzá.

South side of the Painted House, Chichén Itzá.

Following page: Temple of the Warriors and the
Plaza of a Thousand Columns, Chichén Itzá.

Annexe of the Nunnery, Chichén Itzá.

Previous page: Chacmol, Chacmol Temple, Chichén Itzá.

Annexe of the Nunnery and
the Church, Chichén Itzá.

Governor's Palace, Uxmal. In the background the Sorcerer's Pyramid.

The Palace, at Chacmultún, Tekax.

Following page: Temple of the Jaguars, Chichén Itzá.

East side of the Annexe of
the Nunnery, Chichén Itzá.

The Ball Court, Temple of the Jaguars and the Castle, Chichén Itzá.

Following two pages: North corner of the Castle seen from the
Temple of Warriors, Chichén Itzá. In the background, the Ball Court.

Sorcerer's Pyramid, Uxmal.

Previous page: Temple of the Warriors, Chichén Itzá.

Annexe of the Nunnery and the northwest side of the Church, Chichén Itzá.

Temple of the Warriors and the Plaza of a Thousand Columns, Chichén Itzá.

Sabac Ha caves, Tekax.

The Nunnery, Chichén Itzá.

Sabac Ha caves, Tekax.

Previous page: The Church and the
Annexe of the Nunnery, Chichén Itzá.

The Nunnery, Chichén Itzá.

Previous double page: Akab Dzib, Chichén Itzá.

Temple of the Jaguars, Chichén Itzá.

Dragging of the Sacred Cenote, Chichén Itzá.

East side Annexe of the Nunnery, Chichén Itzá.

Governor's Palace, Uxmal.

Temple of the Warriors, Chichén Itzá.

Detail of Serpents' Heads and the skulls of the Tzompantli, Chichén Itzá.

Kikil cenote, Tizimín.

Following page: The Painted
House, Chichén Itzá.

South side of the Observatory, Chichén Itzá.

Detail of the Nunnery, Chichén Itzá.

The Ball Court, Chichén Itzá.

Governor's Palace, Uxmal.

Temple of the Jaguars, Chichén Itzá.

Following page: Detail of
the façade at Labná.

Another view of the dragging of
the Sacred Cenote, Chichén Itzá.

The Castle, Chichén Itzá.

Phallic sculptures, Uxmal.

Previous page: Temple of the Warriors and
the Plaza of a Thousand Columns, Chichén Itzá.

Upper section of the Temple of the Warriors, Chichén Itzá.

West side of the Snail, Chichén Itzá.

West side of the Sorcerer's Pyramid with the Chenes Temple, Uxmal.

Index of Photographs

The number in parentheses is the code allocated to each photograph in the Pedro Guerra photograph archive.

Archaeological Sites of Yucatan
Historical Images.
1st. Edition, 2005.

Producer in chief: Hervé Baeza Braga.
Creative control: Gabriela Calero Cervera.
Graphic design: Alejandra Cárdenas Atoche.
Coordinator of the Pedro Guerra Photographs Archive: Edward Montañez Pérez.
Photographs: Fototeca Pedro Guerra. Facultad de Ciencias Antropológicas. UADY.
Retouched photograph: Christian Pacheco Quijano, Juan Carlos Fleites Góngora.
Introductory texts: Waldemaro Concha Vargas.
Prologue: Lilia Fernández.
Style consultant: Svetlana Larrocha.
Copy checking: Laura Morales Encalada.
Translation: David Phillips.

ISBN: 970-605-330-1
Printed in Mexico.
By Pixel Press S.A. de C.V.